How to Get Followers on Twitter

By Denice Shaw

Copyright Sandy Appleyard-Author 2013

No portion of this work may be reproduced in any way without written consent from the author.

How to Get Followers on Twitter:

A Simple Guide on How to Optimize Twitter and Hootsuite

This book is for both new and experienced Twitter users. The information also applies to writers, small business entrepreneurs, online marketers or just about anyone who wants to gain targeted, loyal followers on Twitter.

How Useful is Twitter?

I've been actively on Twitter for just over a year now and I can honestly say that my life has changed since joining. Nowhere will you find more supportive, generous and helpful people than on Twitter.

My writing career began nearly a decade ago and I never had success at being an author until I joined Twitter. Twitter is the place where I've learned more about social media, writing, book marketing and promotion and so many other useful things I can't even list them. With Twitter, you don't need to surf the internet any more as all the information you would ever need is at your fingertips.

Twitter is where I found my writing coach, editor, beta readers and various other important contacts that I hold very dear to me. Twitter is a place where you'll discover everything you need to know about something, simply by posting a tweet. Imagine 140 characters doing all that!

Without further adieu, I'd like to introduce you to my book, where you'll find everything you need to know to optimize your Twitter usage. I hope you enjoy it!

What you'll find in this book:

-Five easy steps to get massive retweets on Twitter

-Five things you should avoid doing if you want to be successful on Twitter

-How to make a Twitter list and why you should

-Ten simple ways to use your Twitter time wisely

-To follow or not to follow: that is the question

-How productive are Twitter DMs anyway?

-What is Hootsuite and how do you use it?

-Ideas for what to post on Hootsuite

-How to tweet your book-5 easy steps

-What happens when you don't use Hootsuite?

-What Buffer is and why you should use it

-Tweople to follow

-7900 Followers and Still Going Strong

-If You're not Using Buffer Yet, You're Missing Out

-What Makes you Unfollow a Person?

Five Easy Steps to Get Massive Retweets on Twitter

Never have I received more retweets than when I began using one simple rule:

DO NOT THANK FOR RETWEETS!

When I say this, I'm saying literally, DO NOT thank, but do something very simple and productive instead:

RECIPROCATE!!!

DO NOT hit 'reply' at the end of the other person's retweet. Hit their profile and pick the most compelling and recent tweet of theirs and RETWEET IT!!

Here's how:

-Try to find a **direct tweet** (ie. not a retweet). So in my case, most likely my follower is an author. I pick a tweet that relates to their work and retweet it.

-If they do not have a recent original tweet, I **find a tweet or retweet from another author**. (or in your case, whatever your target audience is).

I've said it before and I'll say it again. The most effective way to promote your work is to jump on someone else's promotional band wagon.

-If the follower doesn't have anything recent that relates to their work or another author's work, I retweet something inspirational or interesting.

-If all else fails, I simply say 'thank you' in a tweet.

-Repeat. Watch the retweets pour in!

Before adopting this strategy, I was getting a handful of retweets a day if I was lucky. Now, I get so many I almost can't keep up! My retweets from yesterday alone (without blogging) totaled 40 (and the day wasn't over at the time).

<u>Tip</u>: In order to get massive retweets, be prepared to **tweet regular, compelling and informative tweets.** If my followers are retweeting me and I'm reciprocating, I'll need to have decent tweets to retweet and vice versa, otherwise I'll be following step 4 (and my followers will likely do the same, if not ignore the retweet).

To provide regular tweets, you can use the strategy I've used from '**How to Tweet Your Book-5 Easy Steps**'

Even if you aren't tweeting a book, you can still use the method.

You'll notice that a **loyalty** will form with your regular retweeters. The system will grow and grow and soon become a massive retweeting frenzy with little effort. I found <u>it actually takes less effort to retweet than it does to say thank you</u>, and think about it, aside from being polite, what does thanking really accomplish in Twitter world anyway? **Thanks is better said with action**.

Five Things You Should Avoid Doing if You Want to be Successful on Twitter

My last post was a summary of things you SHOULD do to get lots of returns on Twitter. Here's my take on things you *shouldn't* do:

-Ignore someone who retweets you.

-If someone retweets you, a simple thank you is nice (a retweet is better), even if it's a tweeter who you have absolutely nothing in common with, who isn't even following you. If they retweet you, they did you a favour. You should recognize that.

-Not reciprocating when someone continuously retweets you.

 If you see the same tweeter pop up on retweets more than once, and you've ignored them, that's not proper etiquette. If they have something in common with you (ie. If you're a writer and they too are a writer), you should retweet them back. If not, you should at least thank them.

-Retweeting the same post that someone else retweeted on your behalf.

This is my **number one pet peeve;** when I retweet someone and they simply retweet what I've tweeted, that's double dipping in my opinion, and simply **selfish self promotion** (say that ten times).

-Begging.

Randomly asking someone once to like, subscribe, buy your product or donate to you is fine, but constantly tweeting or making deplorable statements is not going to be very productive . If you want attention, subscribe to the person FIRST, like them FIRST or help support them in some way first, THEN ask for reciprocation.

-Responding Negatively or to Negativity.

Social media is about being social. It's about practicing proper etiquette and meeting new people with similar likes or interests. We all have opinions that we're entitled to, and we're all free to express our different viewpoints. Avoid responding negatively to someone else's ideas. Responding diplomatically with a slightly different angle is perfectly acceptable, but never attack someone for having their take on an issue. Same goes for someone who responds negatively to your posts; either ignore or simply thank them for their comment.

How to Make a Twitter List and Why You Should

Twitter lists are an integral part of staying loyal to your loyal followers. Especially if you are working with many followers (over 1000 is my suggestion).

Here's how Twitter lists work:

-You create a list of all the people on Twitter that you wish to stay on top of (for criteria, see my next post '10 Simple Ways to Use Your Twitter Time Wisely'). I'll get to the instructions momentarily.

-Once you create your list, you view it daily, biweekly, etc. and it will only show you the recent tweets of those you added to your list. Then you can retweet or make mention of all the people you wish in a more timely fashion.

-This is a huge time saver, since you can spend your time only viewing those who have been loyal to you. You can add your loyal tweeters as you go along, and remove any if needed. You can also create a list of tweeters who offer excellent content, even if they do not follow you. That way, you can offer your audience better content without having to search for it.

How to create your list:

-Click on the button that looks like a gear, right beside the 'compose new tweet' button.

-Click on the arrow and select 'Lists'.

-Select 'Create List'. It will give you a menu where you can enter in the name of the list you wish to create.

-Select public or private depending on your preference

(I WOULD SELECT PUBLIC-THIS WAY PEOPLE WILL SEE YOUR LIST AND CAN SUBSCRIBE TO IT IF THEY CHOOSE. THIS ALSO GIVES THE PEOPLE THAT YOU ADD TO YOUR LIST AN OPPORTUNITY TO SEE THAT YOU'VE ADDED THEM, WHICH IS KIND OF LIKE GIVING THEM A PAT ON THE BACK).

-To add people to your list, enter their Twitter name into the field below where you added the list name, OR

-When you're on a person's profile page, the button beside 'following' (the one with the silhouette of a person), select it by clicking on the down arrow and click on 'add or remove from lists'

-To retrieve your list for viewing, simply click on the button that looks like a gear, select 'lists' and click on the list name you want to open.

You can create multiple lists depending on your need. I find this feature very useful, and highly recommend it to anyone who is establishing a platform for anything.

Ten Simple Ways to Use Your Twitter Time Wisely

-Don't just thank or mention new followers. Retweet a post of theirs.

-When people (followers or not) mention or retweet your post, return the favour rather than just thanking them in a mention.

YOU GET NEW FOLLOWERS AND RETWEETS/MENTIONS MULTIPLYING INSTANTLY (PLUS, THANKING, IN MY OPINION IS A TIME WASTER. WHILE POLITE, IT JUST MENTIONS THE PERSON'S NAME, THE READER MUST CLICK AND SEARCH FOR THEIR POSTS.)

-Create a public Twitter list. When followers see you adding them, they may retweet or mention you.

ALSO, IF YOU CREATE A PUBLIC LIST, IT IS VISIBLE TO ALL OF TWITTER (I THINK). POSSIBLY BRINGING MORE FOLLOWERS TO YOU.

Add a person to your public list when they retweet or mention you more than once (especially if they initiated it), it automatically thanks them and others see you've added them, giving them credibility and possible followers.

Use your list to regularly retweet/mention your loyal tweeters, they will likely do the same for you (and it can bring you more followers)

I'm stealing this idea from @NEMultimedia: tweet regularly the posts of the people who influence you the most on Twitter.....better yet, do a blog listing of these tweople and provide reasons why they influenced you.

For more information, see the blog post http://ne-mm.com/5-tweeters-im-thankful-for-and-what-they-taught-me-about-twitter

Don't forget to follow back.

(THIS IS A TRICKY ONE TO SOME-MAKE SURE THEY ARE FAVOURABLE IE. REGULAR TWEETS, INFORMATIVE CONTENT, ETC.)

IF YOU DON'T FOLLOW BACK, YOU RISK LOSING A POTENTIALLY VALUABLE FOLLOWER (ESPECIALLY IF THEY'RE RETWEETING/MENTIONING YOU REGULARLY)

-Use a program like www.justunfollow.com regularly. You can go on every second or third day and remove people who either aren't following you back, or are inactive.

THIS IS ALSO TRICKY FOR SOME, BUT IF YOU WANT TO CONTINUE FOLLOWING BACK YOUR LOYAL FOLLOWERS, YOU'LL NEED TO USE IT.

-<u>Don't ever tweet anything negative</u>. I know this is no secret, but it is advice worth mentioning. Even if you get a negative comment, respond with something positive, like "I'm sorry you feel that way" and leave it alone, or better yet, don't respond at all. This goes double for direct messages, especially the spam I'm sure we all get. Just ignore it all.

-Last but not least, <u>think before you tweet.</u> Think before you retweet. Add <u>value</u> to your posts, so you can gain <u>valuable followers</u>. Make sure you are posting positive, informative, uplifting or funny things. Never EVER rant, insult anyone (including your family-unless it is truly funny and harmless). Negative comments only serve to bring negativity back to you. Surround yourself with positivity.

I've noticed after following all these steps, not only are my followers growing in number (and quality), but I'm also getting better engagement on my website.

To Follow or Not to Follow: That is the Question

I generally follow all my followers, with few exceptions.

I <u>do not</u> follow when:

-It is not a legitimate person. This is determined by a) if they have several tweets, b) if their tweets are legible (some are just lists of twitter handles, or hash tags, not actual language)

Also, if a person doesn't have any followers or very few, yet they are following hundreds, I question if they are real.

-It is NOT someone involved in the pornographic industry. You sometimes have to pull up their profile page to tell (if their website is listed as something vulgar ie. *****.xxx.com or something like that). Sometimes it is blatantly obvious (their profile picture is something you wouldn't show a child)

-It is NOT someone who has several profanities listed in their tweets (or in their twitter name for that matter)

-If it is a blank account. If they have nothing listed on their profile page except a picture and Twitter name, and no website or tweets listed (or very few tweets with nothing on them). Sometimes I've noticed Twitter names to be a bit shady as well. For example, they'll have a bunch of numbers or a combination of letters and numbers with no meaning. I question if that is a real account.

-If it is an account offering something I know I don't want. 5,000 FREE TWITTER FOLLOWERS GUARANTEED!!! You've all seen that one I'm sure. There are others, but that one is the most often seen.

-If the person is English speaking. This is one I debate. I usually look on their profile page and see if they have any English in their tweets. If they don't, I hesitate depending on how many followers they have. It's a tough call for me in this situation, and 9 times out of 10 I follow them anyway. I feel that if they don't provide value, or allow me to provide value to them, I'll unfollow them later. I at least like to give them a chance.

Under any other circumstance, I follow. Even if they aren't writers or authors, or something else that interests me. My feeling is that if they want to follow me, they have something to offer or feel I can offer them something (granted it's something that I'm interested in). If that isn't the case, I'll unfollow them later (using justunfollow.com). But again, I like to give everyone a chance.

After all, you would want everyone to give you a chance, right?

How Productive are Twitter DMs Anyway?

When I began seriously promoting my Twitter account, thus following as many targeted tweople as possible, I noticed I was inundated with DM's, or Direct Messages. Who really reads them? In the beginning, I read and responded to a few but found it very daunting.

As a busy person like everyone else, I'm honestly more inclined to pay more attention to mentions and retweets. Offering thanks with a return mention or retweet is the polite way to give back to your follower, whether new or not.

Direct Messages seem to be a way to self promote tactlessly.

In my opinion, when I follow someone and receive an auto-generated message thanking me (and offering other ways to connect), I feel it is truly thankless. Thank me by following me back or by connecting with me by a retweet or mention. The most infuriating DMs I get are those that are auto-generated to self promote, and you can't even respond because-ha ha- THEY AREN'T FOLLOWING ME BACK!

It was spoken perfectly in a tweet by @Scarberryfields "My getting one of my tweets favorited is like getting roses. RTs & MEs are great! 1 out of my archives-Priceless!xx"

If you truly want to thank someone for following them, send something that everyone will see (like a retweet or mention), not a direct message that only the receiver will see, with a self promoting message attached. Don't get me wrong, simply sending a 'thank you' direct message is fine. But if you're like me, you won't read it.

Use DMs for what they are intended for: personal one-one messages, like sharing an email address so you can communicate further or other personal information that you don't want the whole world to see, or that you don't think the whole world will be interested in.

Chances are you're wasting your time sending DMs, and either you're insulting the receiver or being ignored. I personally have NEVER used DMs unless it was for something personal, and the message was directed to me first (and the sender alerted me on Twitter that I would be receiving it).

What is Hootsuite?

Hootsuite is a wonderful tool for auto-tweeting. It is a vehicle for either syndicating your own content (blogposts, advertisements, reviews, etc.), retweeting a specific message or someone else's, or advertising your own links. The best part is, it is minimal effort, and you don't have to be around to babysit.

How do you use it?

-Simply log on to Hootsuite and register (all you need is an email address and your links to social media sites).

-The main page (getting started) has a box in the middle with different options. The first option you need to select is 'add another social network'.

-Enter the applicable information and suddenly your profile will pop up as a tab on that page. Add in your desired social media sites (I think the free package offers you five, after that you have to pay).

-Once you've completed all your social profiles, you can then schedule tweets by pressing the 'compose message' bar or simply clicking on the 'compose message' field to the upper left of the page.

-Enter in your tweet and then a link (if applicable) by either copying and pasting into the 'add a link' field, or simply typing it in. Then press 'shrink' and it will generate a shortened link with the 'ow.ly' extension.

-Once you're finished, go to the field to the right where it says 'click to select a profile'. When you click on the arrow button, it will show a drop down menu with all your social media icons. Select which one (s) you would like this 'tweet' to be posted to.

-When you're done selecting profiles, you can either click 'send now' or schedule your tweet.

Tip: If this tweet is something you think you'll re-use, hit the 'save' button (looks like a floppy disc) and it will automatically save that message, including the chosen profiles. (If you want to have the choice on profiles each time you send, simply save before selecting your profiles; it will save it without the profiles so you have the option to choose next time you select it).

To select a saved message, hit the arrow key beside the save button and select which message you want. Then follow the steps below.

-To schedule your tweet, you have two options. You can either autoschedule, which lets Hootsuite select the time to post your message depending on when your other messages are placed in the queue, spreading them out in somewhat of an even consistency, or you can schedule the times yourself. I personally prefer this method, that way I can schedule my posts at half hour intervals (or 15 minute intervals, depending on how much traffic I would like to see).

-Press the 'schedule' button (looks like a calendar with the number 30 on it). You'll see the 'autoschedule' button, which you can select by clicking on or leave off. Then you'll see today's date (you don't need to touch this unless you want a schedule a post for another day). You'll also see drop downs for hour and minute and a button for AM and PM.

-Select the time and date you would like to schedule your message to be broadcast and hit 'schedule'

Tip: You can also select 'send me email when message is sent' if you want to ensure you see proof; I used this in the beginning but soon realized it isn't necessary.

-To view your scheduled messages, hit the 'scheduled' button on the left sidebar (looks like a paper airplane). This will show you all your messages, links you've shortened, time it will be sent and which profile(s) the message will be broadcast to.

Tip: Don't select the 'schedule in bulk' button: this is a paid service. If you want many messages scheduled for a couple days, you'll have to do it manually. By using the 'save' button, you can save loads of time retyping messages. I've got about twenty saved messages and I mix them up throughout the day.

Why should you use it?

-To block out the noise.

If you're on a syndicating tribe like I am, or even Triberr, you'll need to ensure you have lots of your own posts popping up on Twitter. If you follow the philosophy that I do (RTs instead of thank yous), if you don't have lots of your content for your followers to RT, you're not going to get a lot of exposure for your own posts.

-To post tweets when you're not available to do it yourself.

Tip: Make sure you're still manually retweeting and connecting with people, otherwise your Twitter account will scream bot, and lose that sense of community. Again, I follow the RT philosophy at least 90% of the time to avoid this issue.

-Save tweets so you can tweet your book or just for advertisements to avoid having to re-type endlessly.

-Shorten links automatically using the shrink button., which saves characters and allows you to expand more on your tweets.

-Keep a tweeting schedule so you can remain consistent.

Tip: Remember to remind yourself to update your Hootsuite schedule, otherwise you'll run out of scheduled tweets and if your community is used to consistent tweets, you'll confuse them and they won't have anything to RT from you!

I've only scratched the surface of what Hootsuite can do in this post. There are endless possibilities, just experiment with the free services, or even sign up for the paid ones, they aren't terribly expensive.

What Should You Schedule on Hootsuite?

My last post: What Hootsuite is, How to Use it and Why you Should Use It' focused on the basics, but with this post, I'd like to focus on different ideas for WHAT to post. I know it seems simple, but I stumbled upon this when I first started, so I thought I would share some ideas to help you out in case you hit a snag.

What Kinds of Posts Should You Schedule?

-A scramble of some or all of your previous blog posts, or your most popular posts (the ones that received the most website traffic).

-A friendly shout out to your followers to like your pages or follow you on other platforms (google, amazon, facebook, etc.)

-Links to book reviews that other authors or reviewers have done for you (don't forget to include a link to their website if it's posted there and their Twitter handle so they get recognition).

-Links to your books promotional sites (Amazon.com, Goodreads, etc.) and a friendly shout out, saying 'Hey, check out my site!'

-Tweet your book (see the next post 'How to Tweet Your Book-5 Easy Steps).

How to Tweet Your Book-Five Easy Steps

We all know how to TWEET, but do we all know how to TWEET A BOOK? It sounds pretty simple, but I have a few little tricks to share.

-**Select excerpts** or favorite lines in your book, copy and paste them into a Word document.

What I also recommend is actually going through your book in chunks, and choosing specific pieces that you think are catchy (without having to read the before part to understand), that will draw your reader's attention.

The first time I did this, I chose about **ten**. Save them all in a Word document and then open up your Hootsuite account. (www.hootsuite.com). If you don't have one, it's really easy to set up, and to start, you only need to set up Hootsuite for Twitter, not for any of the other social media sites.

-**Click on 'compose message'**, select your Twitter profile to your right (to activate the character counter), and begin typing in your first excerpt. You'll have to play around and edit your excerpt to fit into the allowable number of characters. This is why I only chose ten to start.

-Cut and paste the link to Amazon.com or wherever your book is available into the 'add a link' field and click on 'shrink'. You can even do this before you add your excerpt since the link will take up characters and you'll have to re-edit afterwards.

-**Click on the save button** (looks like a floppy disc). This will save your excerpt including your link and Twitter profile into your drafts.

-Click on the calendar to **schedule your tweet**. Continue doing this with all your excerpts until you have a nice collection to get started.

Once you have your ten excerpts saved in drafts, all you have to do is click on the arrow beside the save button to retrieve them. You can schedule them as often as you like (I did mine every half hour). I also recommend tweeting your short pitch and links to any promotional websites your book can be found on as well.

Tip: Don't forget to schedule Tweets **around the clock**. There are people all over the world in **different time zones** who may catch your tweets!

I found that once I had a nice pattern of tweets, I also received a nice influx of **retweets** from my audience. To gain return on those, be sure to return the favor and **retweet back**. **JUMPING ON ANOTHER AUTHOR'S**

PROMOTIONAL BAND WAGON IS THE BEST WAY TO RECEIVE MORE RETWEETS AND SUPPORT.

<u>Tip</u>: You can also use Hootsuite to post your book excerpts into <u>other social media sites</u>, you don't have to just use Twitter!

What Happens When You Don't Use Hootsuite?

Have you ever wondered what would happen if you didn't use Hootsuite? If you didn't have any of your OWN content circulating for a period of time?

I conducted a little experiment recently. <u>The experiment's purpose was twofold:</u> **1)** I needed to take a little vacation from things, and **2)** I wanted to perform an experiment to see what would happen if I didn't use Hootsuite and thus, didn't re-post any of my own material.

The content circulating on my Twitter account was simply from Buffer and the syndicating tribe I'm involved in. Therefore **none of my own posts were advertised**.

So what happened?

-My rate of new followers dropped (not significantly but it was notable)

-Mentions declined drastically, almost to a halt

What does this mean?

-That I have very loyal Tweeters who prefer to only tweet my own content

-The people who follow me prefer more of a <u>personal and intimate</u> tweeter who often tweets their own stuff

-If I can be so bold as to say this: PERHAPS my Tweeters feel that my posts are more enjoyable? More informative? They GET MORE RETURN from retweeting just my posts?

This is kind of bad news for tribes though; DOES THIS MEAN THAT RETWEETING OTHER PEOPLE'S STUFF IS FROWNED UPON? Perhaps RETWEETS FROM OTHER SOURCES DON'T GET AS GOOD A RETURN? **What do you think?**

Once I began using Hootsuite together with Buffer again I noticed things returned to normal. I did decide that I was getting the **best return on my posts by re-posting slightly less frequently**. My point is this: it doesn't hurt to **try something new** and see what difference it makes. You never know, with just a SLIGHT TWEAK, YOU CAN MAKE A HUGE DIFFERENCE. Don't be afraid to try something for a few days to see what happens!

What Buffer is and Why You Should Use It

I'm a writer, and like all writers I'm trying to establish my platform. My most successful social media outlet to date is Twitter. I've spent countless hours retweeting people who have mentioned my posts or retweeted me.

My philosophy is this: don't thank people by simply saying thank you, thank them by retweeting or mentioning them, you'll get way more out of that and so will your tweeps.

In doing this, I found I was extremely overwhelmed. Up until about three weeks ago, I was spending up to 3 hours a day retweeting people. It snowballed from one or two retweets to OVER 100 A DAY; which is absolutely wonderful and very exciting. But this left one problem: **I didn't have time for much else.**

Until I found a little program called Buffer. With Buffer, you can schedule your retweets and mentions for specific times of the day (similar to Hootsuite) only unlike Hootsuite, Buffer is essentially for use on websites like Twitter. It doesn't work well if you want to retweet your own material, for that stick with Hootsuite.

Buffer is great in that it gives you the opportunity to have **retweets around the clock**. You don't have to babysit. There is no need to hop on Twitter for hours at a time and simply retweet people. You can go on whenever you want, select the retweets you want and walk away. Let Buffer do the rest. The program will ensure that your retweets and mentions are posted in increments so you have a constant flow around the clock.

The best thing about it is that <u>when your tweets are getting low it sends you an email</u> saying that you need to top it up. It also **inserts the person's handle whom you're retweeting** so they'll know you're retweeting them. It's a win win situation.

<u>It couldn't be easier to set up either</u>. It's literally a few clicks and you're done. All it is is a SEPARATE BUTTON BESIDE YOU'RE RETWEET BUTTON when you're on Twitter, so you can either choose to retweet now or add to your Buffer.

If you want the free version (trial) you'll have about 10 retweets to play with. If you're successful on Twitter that won't be enough. The good news is that the **paid version is only $10 a month**. In my opinion, it's money well spent. Ever since using the program I'm <u>saving loads of time each day and best of all my followers are multiplying with little effort</u>.

Coupled with Hootsuite, Buffer is an essential program if you want to be successful on Twitter. I highly recommend it; not only is it easy and affordable, but it'll save you tons of time, trust me.

Tweople to Follow

The following list is from my own Twitter list of loyal followers. These are the people who have helped me get to where I am on Twitter and other social media platforms. You don't have to follow them, but I highly recommend them if you're looking for some loyalty. (especially if you're a writer-most of these people are also writers)

@LawrenceWray

@JacksonArthurUS

@Jason_Bournesm

@MichaelJMcCann1

@KatieMettner

@ChandlerMcGrew

@SandyCally

@JohnDolanAuthor

@Davepperlmutter

@danielkemp6

@JoyceDeBacco

@markcoruk

@growwithstacy

@vgrefer

@Bestdietbook

@KRRowe

@authorAVBarber

@g2lmel

__7900 Followers and Going Strong…How?__

For some of you, 7900 followers is A DROP IN THE BUCKET.

But for others, the number may seem overwhelming. It's not really that difficult. The key is **reciprocation** and **consistency**.

__Reciprocation says so many things about you as a Twitter user.__

-You're loyal.

-You're polite (it's a simple, yet effective way to say THANK YOU).

-Sharing quality content is important to you (and you're not afraid to share your own knowledge).

-You want to help others who have helped you.

-You don't discriminate.

-You're not driven by your ego.

-You're a hard worker, and you're not just here for a free ride.

So, how do you reciprocate? Besides the obvious.

-Join a syndication tribe.

-Start a Twitter list and draw tweets from your loyal followers.

-Use Buffer, Hootsuite or Tweetdeck to spread your tweets out (and to avoid getting held in Twitter prison).

-Join Triberr and blog regularly.

Tip: Make sure you log into Twitter at least once a day or once every second day to avoid getting behind in your reciprocating tweets.

In the beginning, I found myself spending HOURS EACH DAY striving for new followers. <u>Randomly following people</u> generally <u>didn't work for me</u>. If you find you're going weeks with just a sprinkling of new followers here and there, don't fret.

It's better to gain and maintain loyal new followers, no matter how seldom they come.

Having a loyal following means
being patient and kind, working hard and often.

Never underestimate the power of Twitter. If YOU WANT TO BE NOTICED, share valuable knowledge often, from your work and from others. Once you're regularly contributing to the Twitter environment, you'll notice how HELPFUL the site is. Not just in terms of the plethora of available information, but in the people you'll meet.

So get Tweeting!

If You're not Using Buffer Yet, You're Missing Out

It all started out with about 5000 followers on my Twitter account. That was approximately four or five months ago.

Now I'm at over 8000 followers and still going strong. I have a little secret to making this happen: Buffer

What is Buffer? What does it do?

Buffer is an application used for spreading out your Twitter tweets. What it enables you to do is <u>select any number of tweets</u> (tweets, retweets or mentions) FROM YOUR TWITTER STREAM FOR RETWEETING AT A LATER TIME. It helps you spread them out to avoid having your account frozen and ending up in the proverbial 'Twitter jail'.

Why is this Useful?

Well, as mentioned above, it allows you to <u>choose which times you'd like to post</u> your tweets. You can also <u>'mix them up'</u> so they're not just posting in the order which you selected them in. This is useful because you're NOT FORCED to have multiple tweets posted all at the same time, and it also **helps free you from having to spend hours per day on Twitter**; you can simply maintain your supply of tweets throughout any number of days.

What other uses does it have?

For someone who has MULTIPLE TWITTER ACCOUNTS (since I'm an author and I write under different names and genres), it enables me to post my tweets to several accounts at a time, so <u>I don't have to segregate one account</u> and then spend the same amount of time on my other accounts. You can also SELECT OR DESELECT FROM YOUR ACCOUNTS IF A PARTICULAR POST DOESN'T APPLY to all of them.

Why is this Helpful?

-You can potentially gain more followers in multiple accounts simply by retweeting to one or all of your accounts.

-It is a HUGE time saver!

-Followers will see you as more of an asset, since you have multiple accounts and they know that you can potentially post their tweets to one or all of your accounts, gaining them more exposure.

-Buffer allows you to post unlimited amounts of tweets to several accounts (this also includes Facebook, Google and LinkedIn accounts) with the paid option.

-Buffer is free for the first ten or so tweets per day, but after that, it's only TEN DOLLARS a month! Think of the amount of time it'll save you for a mere ten bucks!

It's no wonder Buffer has over one million users. Here is an excerpt of an article from AppStorm entitled 'Buffer: A Second Look':

"I was incredibly pleased with the new and revamped Buffer. During the initial stages of the app's development when I reviewed it last time, it seemed that the app was more targeted at businesses and professionals and though I agree that this is probably the app's most logical demographic, the developers have progressed the app to a stage now where I can see the appeal for everyday users of the social networking websites that just want a way to share things when they don't have time to actively post updates but want to maintain their online presence. The revamp of the design certainly helps to cement this and I think the team have come on in leaps and bounds in terms of taking a fairly averagely-designed app and turning it into something that people enjoy using. All in all, the new Buffer is incredible."

After using Buffer for the last five months, I can honestly say that it has saved my life social media-wise. This is not an affiliated post, I have not been paid to say anything here; this is the honest truth. It is a very big help and definitely WORTH THE TEN DOLLAR SACRIFICE. Plus, it's so easy to use and their customer service is better than anywhere else in my opinion.

So if you're struggling with Twitter and trying to keep up, or if you find your number of followers to be dwindling, I highly recommend trying Buffer.

What Makes you Unfollow a Person?

We've all had to do it. It is just as easy to **follow** a person as it is to **unfollow**, but what makes us CLICK THAT BUTTON to get rid of someone?

I've discussed reasons to follow or not to follow, but now I'd like to explore the reasons we unfollow.

Personally, I do it very rarely, especially on Facebook, where I have extremely loyal followers and a lot less of them compared to what I have on Twitter.

Recently I unfollowed a Facebook follower and felt badly about it. This person had been following me (and still is) for well over a year, but they continued to POST PICTURES THAT I JUST COULDN'T STOMACH ANYMORE.

Here is a list of reasons why I unfollow:

 -Posting inappropriate pictures (mentioned above)

-Posting offensive content (racial, sexist, etc.)

-Boring posts or posts with no real point

-Posts about trivial things (what I ate for dinner, etc.)

-Regularly posting about drinking, partying or sex (I'm okay if it's once in a while)

-Personal attacks on people

-Posting <u>content</u> that is no longer applicable or useful to me or my audience (non-sharable)

-Posting spam

-Regularly posting <u>links</u> that aren't useful to me or my audience

-Overly driven posts about causes/constant preaching about causes

-Posts that are gross (vomiting, blood, personal hygiene, etc.)

-Regular use of bad language (I don't mind a little if it's poignant)

-Constant negativity or complaining (it's different if the post has a thought-provoking point but initially is negative)

Most of these items can be handled on an occasional basis. <u>I have never deleted somebody</u> because of one single offensive/distasteful post. I think it's important to KEEP AN OPEN MIND today, especially when dealing with social media. <u>We all have different opinions</u> and we all need to respect them.

Conclusion

I've been using all of the above tips for over a year and have found a lot of success on Twitter. The other things that play a part are quality content, reciprocation and consistency. The more often you provide these things, the more returns you'll get on social media.

The most important thing to remember is you must share. Share your knowledge, share the knowledge you find when you do research, and share the Twitter handles of the most helpful and influential people that you find. When you do these things, you'll be more of an asset to your followers and your current followers will become more loyal and respectful of your tweets.

It's also worth mentioning that you must be sure to put a cap on self promotion. Too much of it will turn followers away since you won't be much of an asset to them, and it will look like that's the only reason you're on Twitter. A healthy balance is found when you utilize both Hootsuite for your own posts and Buffer for others' posts.

Show that you have a personality. People will be more inclined to follow, mention and retweet posts that are meaningful, helpful, inspirational and/or funny. You don't always have to be serious when you tweet. Sometimes putting a smile on someone's face is as simple as telling a quick joke or saying something poignant. It's the a-propos things that I tweet sometimes that touch people who wouldn't normally respond.

In my opinion, Twitter is more advantageous to me as a writer than any other social media platform. It has brought more traffic to my website than any other referrer. One of the best things about Twitter is once you hit a point where all your followers know you and what you do on Twitter regularly, it becomes less work. I read this fact from Chuck Sambuchino's 'Create Your Writer Platform' and at the time I didn't believe it.

Please don't ever fall for the fly by night "Get 500 Twitter followers" gimmicks, either. I never did but from what I've heard, yes you do get the followers, but they're not loyal and certainly not targeted. If you need your ego padded that badly, you're in the wrong business.

Building a solid social media platform takes time and effort, there are no cutting corners. I can honestly say that I've been actively on Twitter for over a year and to date I have 7000 followers. Every follower has been rightfully earned. You lose followers some days and you gain some, but most importantly they come to you for what you have to offer and what they can offer you. There are no one way streets in social media. Unless you're a celebrity, this strategy will lead to failure.

Put a little effort into building your Twitter platform each day and I guarantee if you follow the advice I've given you in this book, you'll be successful.

I hope all this advice helped.

Also check out:

INDIE WRITING ADVICE

A Simple Guide on Writing and Optimizing Your Social Media Platform

DENICE SHAW

Click here to purchase:
http://www.amazon.com/dp/B00CPL637Q

And:

INDIE WRITING ADVICE

A Simple Guide for Sharpening Your Writing Skills, Platform Building, and Submitting to Publishers

DENICE SHAW

Click here to purchase: http://www.amazon.com/dp/B00J7YSLI8

www.ingramcontent.com/pod-product-compliance
Lightning Source LLC
Chambersburg PA
CBHW071602170526
45166CB00004B/1758